Malacology

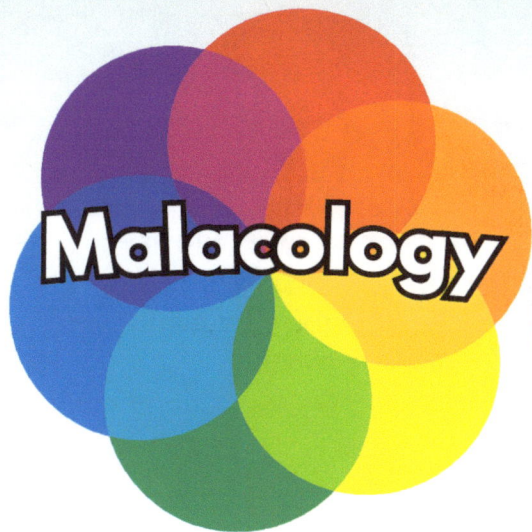

Book of COLORS
A Rainbow of Mollusks

Jessica Lee Anderson

Paperback ISBN: 978-1-964078-48-9

To Ava, Elizabeth, and Miriam, I hope you continue to love learning always! Follow your dreams! - JLA

Mollusks are often multi-colored, so have fun pointing out the variety of colors in addition to the featured colors! Photos are not to scale.

Photo credits, left to right, top to bottom: Front cover: Divelvanov (Coconut octopus); ; Interior cover: Mikelillo (Polka-dot chromodorid); Copyright page: Xiao Zhou (Candy cane snail shell), Iaroslav Borisovskyi (Giant African snail); Dedication page: glucosala; p. 4: Howard Chen, cascoly, Edward Snow; p. 5: Jacob Philip, Mblain93, Michel Viard; p. 6: Martin Voeller, kipgodi, atese; p. 7: Whitepointer, joebelanger, atese; p. 8: RibeirodosSantos, Gerald Corsi, Alina Rodgers; p. 9: FishTales, fotograv, richcarey; p. 10: Rytis Bernotas, Jamaludin Yusup, MarineKing; p. 11: wrangel, TMarantette, colimachon; p. 12: Rob Atherton, vlad61, S.Rohrlach; p. 13: AnjoKanFotografie, AlexeyMasliy, Serhii Klizub; p. 14: LagunaticPhoto, S.Rohrlach, ultramarinfoto; p. 15: Dmitry Rukhlenko, Rob Atherton, chrupka; p. 16: PsarevaOlga, Michael Zeigler, Taveesaksri; p. 17: S-A-J, Michael Zeigler, Global_Pics; p. 18: bagi1998, gyro, Kevin Wells; p. 19: wrangel, Marie Carr, BZH22; p. 20: Kesterhu, Eduardo Baena, Cavan Images; p. 21: naturediver, HHelene, ifish; p. 22: Velvetfish, Flicketti, Gelpi; p. 23: CHIBICCOclub, y-studio, elfpdl33; p. 24: Nigel Marsh, Sergey Shcherbakov, Gerald Corsi; p. 25: atese,_pclark2, VitalisG; p. 26: Stéphane ROCHON, optionm, David_Slater; p. 27: Giorgio Cavallaro, wademcmillan, Aitor Diaz; p. 28: FishTales, Subaqueosshutterbug, Divelvanov; p. 29: chengyuzheng, milachirolde, scubaluna; 30: Trueog, John Anderson Photo, Rob Atherton; p. 31: peilien, AndamanSE, LagunaticPhoto; p. 32: FishTales, S.Rohrlach, Norman Lopez; p. 33: AndamanSE, johnandersonphoto, Aneese; p. 34: Michael Anderson; Back cover: Vojce (Maxima clam)

This Book Belongs to:

_____

Malacology is the study of mollusks like clams, chitons, nautiluses, octopuses, oysters, slugs, snails, and squids.

Chambered nautilus

Red

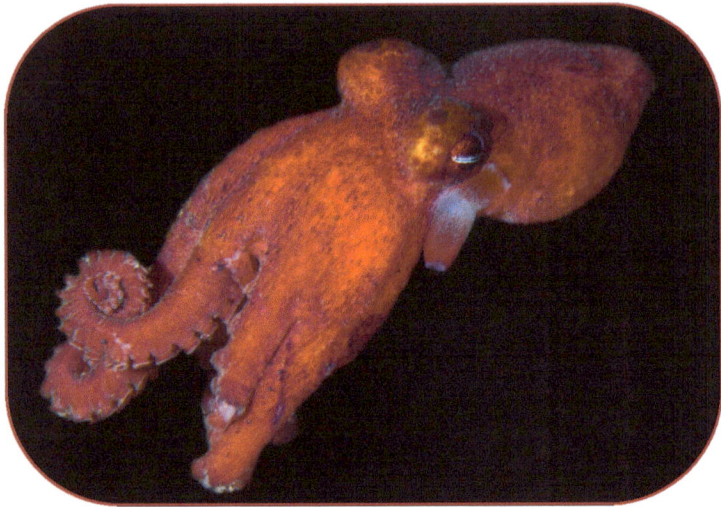
Pygmy octopus

Gumboot chiton

Mollusks (molluscs) are animals with soft bodies and no backbones (invertebrates).

Red nudibranch

Red

Pharoah cuttlefish

Mollusks come in many shapes and colors. Some species such as cuttlefish, squids, and octopuses can even change colors!

Strawberry top shells

Red slug

5

Orange

North Pacific giant octopus

Orange slug

Mollusks range in length from snails the size of a sharp pencil tip to the giant squid that is longer than a school bus.

White-and-orange-tipped nudibranch

Orange

Short-tailed nudibranch

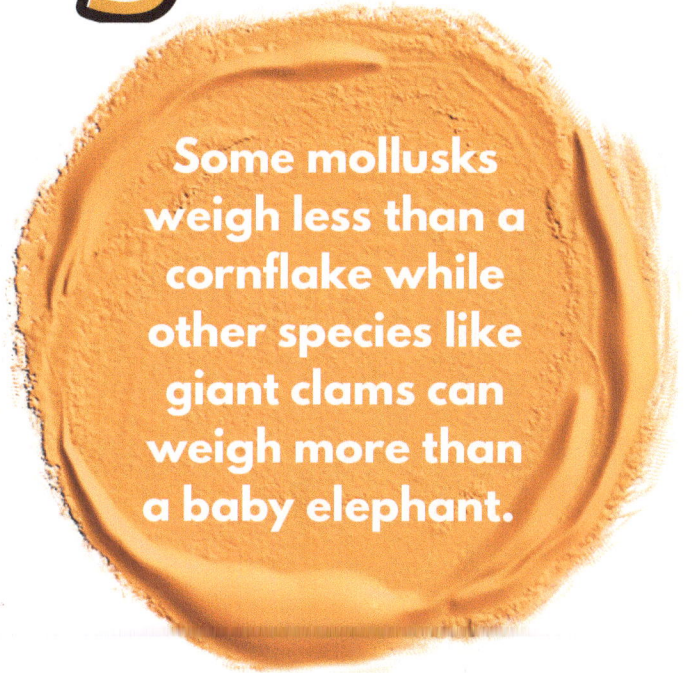

Some mollusks weigh less than a cornflake while other species like giant clams can weigh more than a baby elephant.

Hairy octopus

Flame shell

Yellow

Mototi octopus

Bigfin reef squid

Cuttlefish, squids, nautiluses, and octopuses are a class of mollusks known as cephalopods.

Banana slug

Yellow

Wedge clam

Many mollusk species like clams, oysters, and snails have a protective shell made from calcium carbonate.

Many-lobed nudibranch

Pharoah cuttlefish

Green

Green-lipped mussels

Emerald green snail

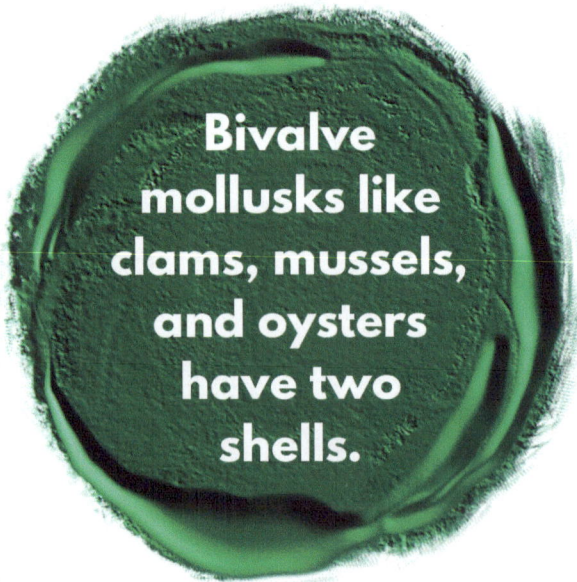

Bivalve mollusks like clams, mussels, and oysters have two shells.

Lettuce sea slug

Green

Triton's trumpet snail

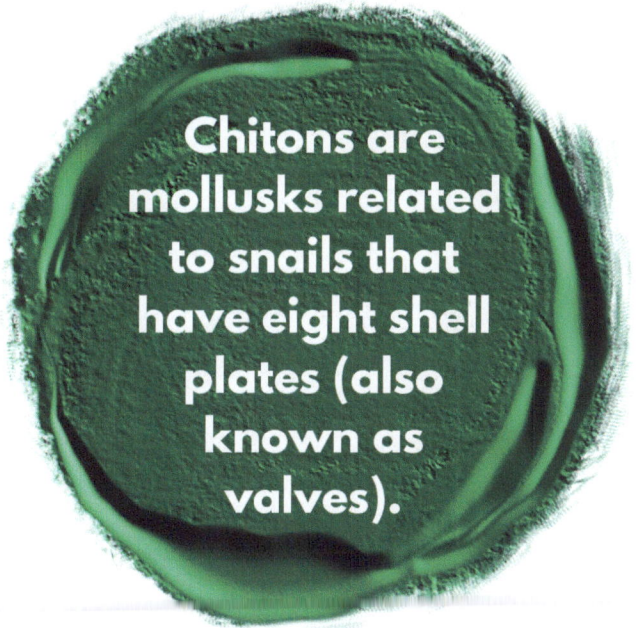

Chitons are mollusks related to snails that have eight shell plates (also known as valves).

Pharaoh cuttlefish

Green chiton

Blue

There are over 85,000 mollusk species found all over the world, including Antarctica!

Bobtail squid

Giant clam

Blue dragon (sea slug)

Blue

Blue mussels

Common octopus

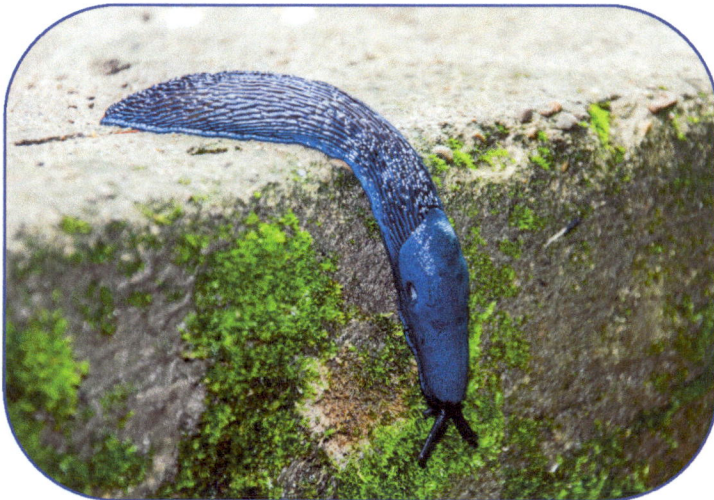
Blue slug

Gastropods like snails and slugs are a diverse, widespread class of mollusks.

Purple

Dwarf cuttlefish

Gloomy octopus

Some mollusks like octopuses have venom—a toxic secretion used for hunting and defense. Many nudibranchs are poisonous.

Purple nudibranch

Purple

Common European cuttlefish

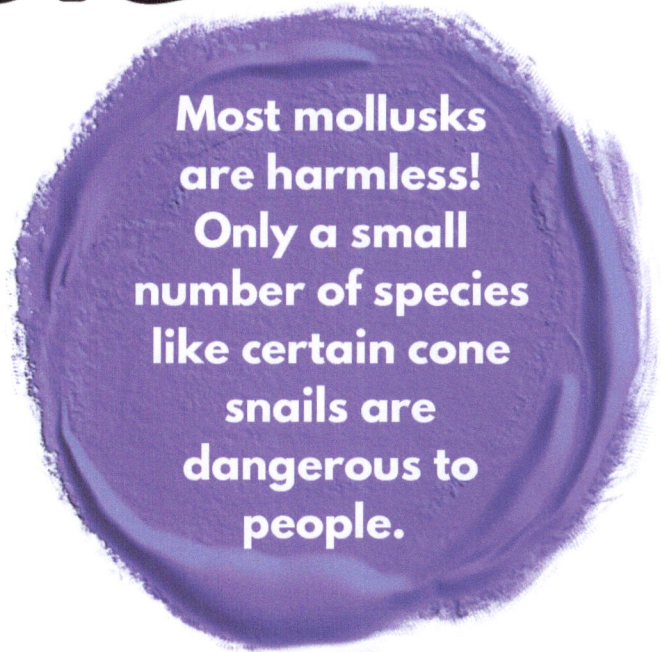

Most mollusks are harmless! Only a small number of species like certain cone snails are dangerous to people.

Purple lady nudibranch

Violet sea snail

Pink

North Pacific giant octopus

Bigfin reef squid

Most mollusks are marine, meaning they are found in and around the ocean.

Pink conch

Pink

Ramshorn snail

Mollusk species can also be found in freshwater and on land (terrestrial).

Hopkin's rose nudibranch

Carribean reef squid

Black

Sea snails

Black abalone

Certain mollusks dine on algae, fungi, and plants (herbivores). Other species feed on other animals (carnivores).

Otway black snail

Black

Common octopus

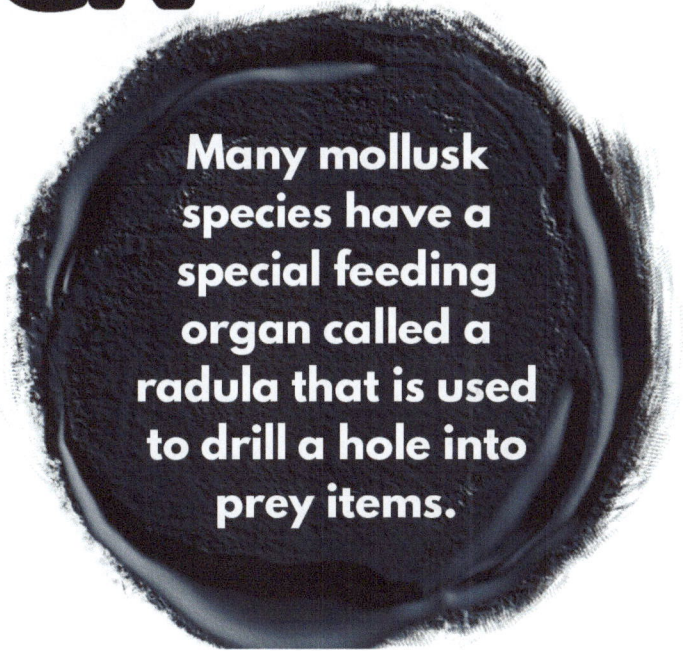

Many mollusk species have a special feeding organ called a radula that is used to drill a hole into prey items.

Black slug

Black mussels

White

Black-eyed squids

Alabaster nudibranch

Mollusk species like squid and octopuses can swim while other species like sea slugs creep around using a muscular foot.

Pacific red octopus

White

Hudson's horned dorid nudibranch

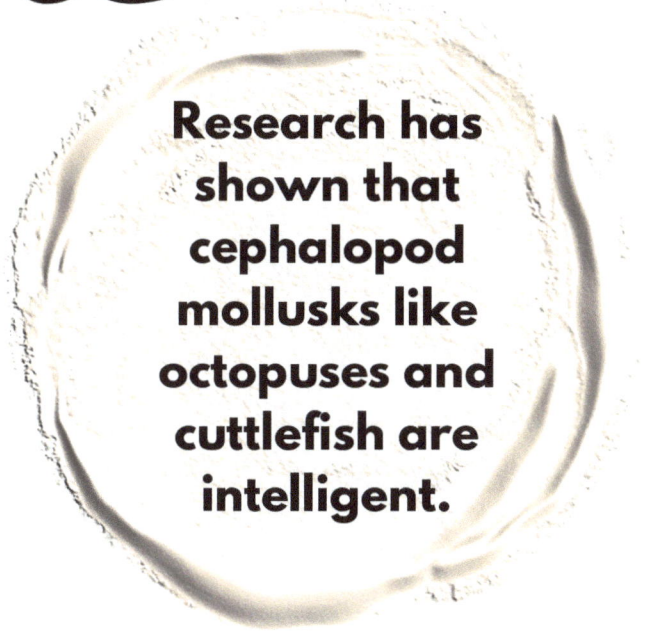

Research has shown that cephalopod mollusks like octopuses and cuttlefish are intelligent.

Venus comb murex snail

Pharaoh cuttlefish

Gray

Long-arm octopus

Broadclub cuttlefish

A group of octopuses is called a tangle, and a group of snails is called a rout or walk.

Gray clam

Gray

Gray slugs

Scientists are continuing to discover new mollusk species and learn more about them.

Ark clams

Scallops

Brown

Giant cuttlefish

Eastern oysters

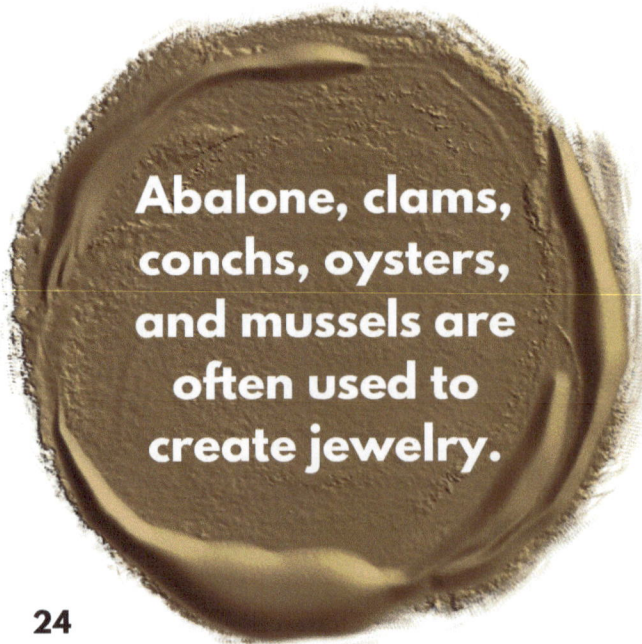

Abalone, clams, conchs, oysters, and mussels are often used to create jewelry.

California two-spot octopus

Brown

Coconut octopus

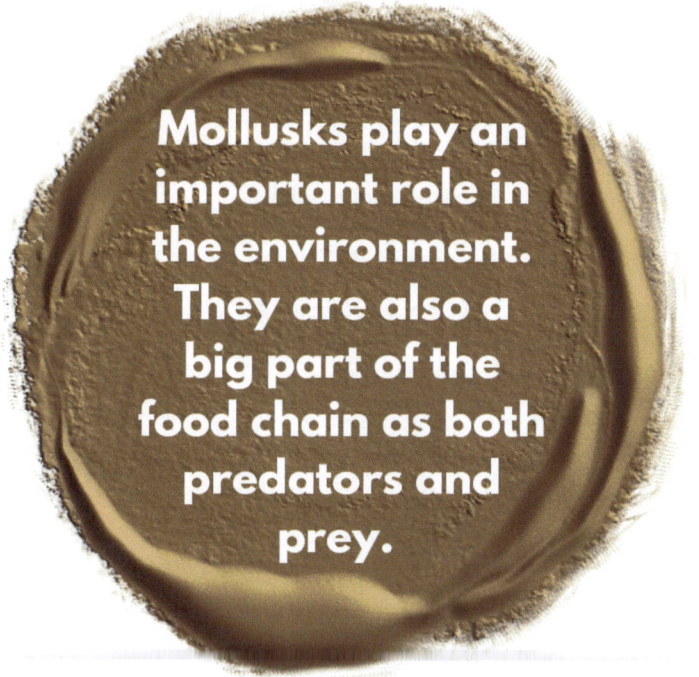

Mollusks play an important role in the environment. They are also a big part of the food chain as both predators and prey.

Carribean reef squid

Great pond snail

COLOR Combinations

What do you notice about these squid patterns and colors?

Hummingbird bobtail squid

Hummingbird bobtail squid

Hawaiian bobtail squid

COLOR Combinations

Wandering cratena nudibranch

Spanish shawl nudibranch

Pikachu nudibranch

What are some things you notice about the shapes, colors, and features of these nudibranchs?

COLOR Combinations

What are some colors and features you notice about these mollusks?

Flamboyant cuttlefish

Blue-ringed octopus

Mosaic octopus

COLOR Combinations

Conchs

Painted snail

Cone snail

What do these shells have in common? How are they different?

COLOR Combinations

Can you describe the colors, patterns, and features of these octopuses?

Mimic octopus

Carribean coral garden octopus

Starry night octopus

COLOR Combinations

Chambered nautilus

Pygmy cuttlefish

Wonderpus octopus

Can you describe the shapes and colors of these mollusks? Why do you think they're different?

COLOR Combinations

Can you describe the colors and patterns of these marine mollusks?

Variable neon slug

Clown nudibranch

Miniature melo sea snail

COLOR Combinations

Little egg cowrie

Flamingo tongue snail

Tiger cowrie

Why do you think the colors, shapes, and features of a shell matters?

Jessica Lee Anderson is an award-winning author of over 100 books for young readers including the NAOMI NASH chapter book series. Jessica loves spending time in nature and exploring the outdoors with her husband, Michael, and their daughter, Ava! Jessica loves admiring mollusks (especially when snorkeling in Hawaii). You can learn more about Jessica by visiting www.jessicaleeanderson.com.

Check out these other books:

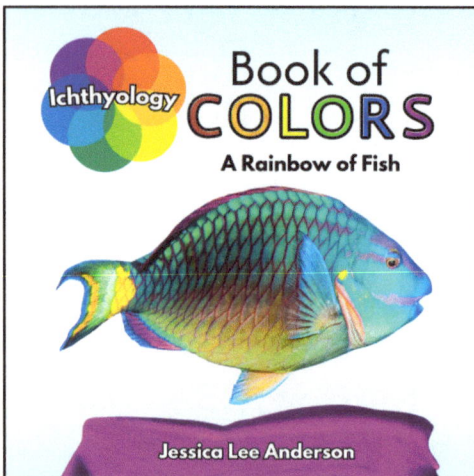

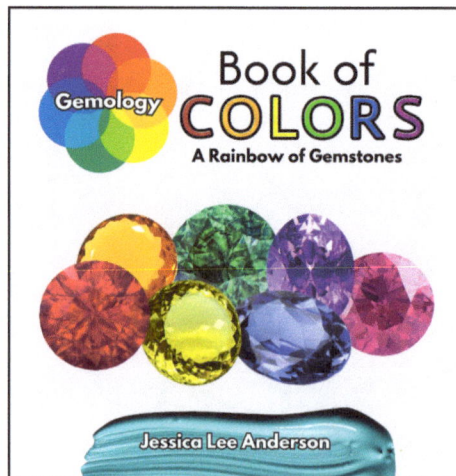

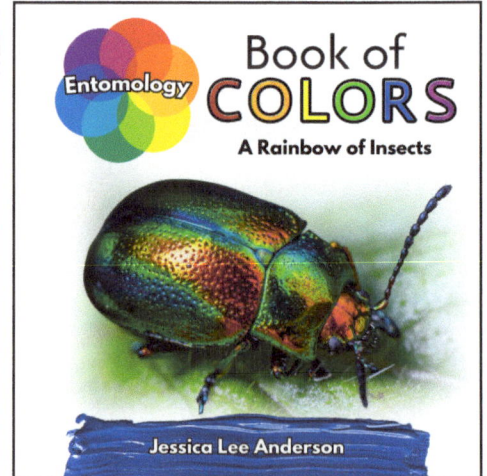

Ichthyology
Book of COLORS
A Rainbow of Fish
Jessica Lee Anderson

Gemology
Book of COLORS
A Rainbow of Gemstones
Jessica Lee Anderson

Entomology
Book of COLORS
A Rainbow of Insects
Jessica Lee Anderson

www.ingramcontent.com/pod-product-compliance
Lightning Source LLC
Chambersburg PA
CBHW061145030426
42335CB00002B/104